LET'S TALK ABOUT
COLLEGE

── THE 10 STEPS TO ──

UNLOCKING
OPPORTUNITIES FOR

FIRST GENERATION COLLEGE
ADMISSIONS

How to unveil your unique narrative, build a strong academic profile, master your personal statement and more!

KATINA FOSTER

TABLE OF CONTENTS

INTRODUCTION

Meet Katina Foster, a seasoned professional with over 20 years of experience in transportation logistics. Katina is a dedicated single parent to two academically accomplished teenage sons. As the family navigated the challenging journey of first-gen college admissions with their oldest, they encountered obstacles in finding relevant information. Undeterred, they combed into extensive research, transforming their experience into an invaluable resource – an ebook designed to guide others through the intricacies of the college acceptance process.

Proudly witnessing their eldest son's acceptance into several colleges, Katina is now passionate about helping others on a similar path. Drawing from personal triumphs and challenges, Katina is committed to empowering individuals and ensuring the journey to college acceptance becomes achievable for all.

Join us on a powerful journey into the workings of securing your spot in college, an important part of our five-step blueprint for acceptance. This journey is the heart of the matter – a carefully laid-out, step-by-step process designed to be your key to unlocking the door of opportunity. From crafting compelling applications to mastering interviews, each stage is thoughtfully presented with actionable insights and resources. Picture the impact on your life – confidence gained, doors opened, and the path to a brighter future illuminated. Your journey to college acceptance begins here, and we're here to guide you every step of the way.

STEP 1: UNVEILING YOUR UNIQUE NARRATIVE

The first crucial step is crafting a compelling application that tells your unique story. It's not about grades and scores; it's about showcasing the qualities, experiences, and perspectives that make you stand out. Dive into self-reflection to unearth your passions, challenges, and triumphs. This self-reflection is the foundation upon which your entire application will rest – a narrative that captivates and resonates with admissions officers.

Crafting Your Compelling Application - Unveiling Your Unique Narrative

In college admissions, your application is not just a piece of paper; it's your canvas to paint a vivid picture of who you are beyond grades and scores. It's an opportunity to tell your unique story that captivates and resonates with admissions officers. This chapter unveils the crucial first step in your journey – crafting a compelling application that reveals the narrative that defines you.

Unearthing the Essence: Beyond Grades and Scores

The journey begins with a shift in perspective. No longer confined by numbers on a transcript or standardized test scores. You step into a realm where your essence takes center stage on a transcript or standardized test scores. Your application is your narrative, and it's time to unveil the layers that define you.

Unearthing the Essence: Beyond Grades and Scores

The journey begins with a shift in perspective. No longer confined by numbers on a transcript or standardized test scores, you step into a realm where your essence takes center stage. Your application is your narrative, and it's time to unveil the layers that define you.

Seeing Beyond the Surface: Self-Reflection as the Catalyst

Self-reflection becomes your compass, guiding you through the labyrinth of your experiences, passions, challenges, and triumphs. Picture it as a journey through the corridors of your mind, where you excavate the moments that shaped you. It's about seeing beyond the surface, peeling back the layers to reveal the core of your identity.

Embracing Your Passions: The Heartbeat of Your Narrative

Passions are the heartbeat of your narrative – the rhythm that resonates with authenticity. Picture admissions officers immersing themselves in your story, feeling the pulse of your enthusiasm for what truly matters to you. Whether art, science, community service, or any other pursuit, your passions infuse life into your application, making it memorable and compelling.

Confronting Challenges: The Canvas of Resilience

As you unveil your narrative, acknowledge the challenges that shaped you. This is not about showcasing a flawless facade but embracing the authenticity of your journey. Admissions officers appreciate resilience, the ability to face challenges head-on and emerge stronger. They want to see the canvas of your resilience, painted with strokes of determination and lessons learned.

Celebrating Triumphs: The Bright Strokes of Achievement

Triumphs are the bright strokes that illuminate your narrative. Whether it's academic achievements, personal milestones, or overcoming obstacles, each triumph contributes to the masterpiece of your application. Picture admissions officers recognizing your capacity for success, resilience, and growth – a narrative that invites them to envision your potential on their campus.

Crafting the Narrative: The Art of Authentic Storytelling

Now, let's delve into the art of crafting this narrative. Imagine weaving a story that captures attention from the first sentence. It's not about embellishments or elaborate language; it's about authenticity and resonance. Your narrative should mirror your true self

– a story that admissions officers connect with on a personal level.

Seeing, Feeling, Experiencing: The Admissions Officer's Journey

Envision the admissions officer stepping into your narrative, seeing the vivid scenes, feeling the emotions, and experiencing the moments that define you. Your words become a portal, transporting them into your world. Create an immersive experience where they understand your journey and feel compelled to be part of the chapter you're about to unfold on their campus.

Amplifying Emotional Impact: The Power of Connection

As you craft your narrative, amplify the emotional impact. It's not about relying on jargon or clichés; it's about creating a genuine connection. Allow admissions officers to feel the heartbeat of your story – the excitement of your passions, the resilience in the face of challenges, and the joy of triumphs. Emotions resonate, and it's these resonances that elevate your narrative.

Direct, Engaging, Authentic: Your Voice in Every Word

Your voice is the guiding force in this narrative. Be direct, engaging, and authentic in every word. Imagine the clarity of your voice cutting through the noise, making your story impossible to ignore. Avoid the temptation of elaborate language; simplicity and authenticity are your allies.

The Unveiling: Your Narrative as a Living, Breathing Entity

As you complete this chapter, visualize your narrative as a living, breathing entity, ready to step off the pages of your application. It's not just about submitting documents; it's about presenting a piece of yourself – a narrative that has the power to linger in the minds of admissions officers.

Conclusion: Your Unique Narrative Awaits Unveiling

In conclusion, this chapter is your guide to unveiling the narrative that defines you. It's a journey of self-discovery, authenticity, and connection. Your passions, challenges, and triumphs are not just components of an application but the colors that paint your unique canvas. As you embark on this journey, remember that your narrative is not a static tale but a dynamic force ready to captivate and resonate.

STEP 2: BUILDING A STRONG ACADEMIC PROFILE

While grades aren't the sole determinant of success, a solid academic profile is undeniably important. This step delves into strategies for maintaining a competitive GPA, selecting challenging courses, and seeking support when needed. Your academic journey is a key aspect of your application, and this step ensures you present it in the best light possible.

Building a Strong Academic Profile - Nurturing Your Path to Success

Your academic profile takes center stage in the intricate dance of college admissions. While grades don't hold the exclusive key to success, they undeniably play a pivotal role. This chapter unfolds strategies to maintain a competitive GPA, navigate the labyrinth of course selection, and seek support when needed. Your academic journey is a canvas, and this step ensures you paint it in the best light possible.

The Academic Odyssey: Navigating Your Journey

Picture your academic journey as an odyssey, each semester a new chapter in the epic of your education. It's not just about the grades you attain; it's about the growth, challenges, and resilience embedded in your academic narrative. Let's embark on this odyssey, ensuring each step strengthens your academic profile.

The Competitive GPA: A Beacon of Academic Excellence

Your GPA is not just a number; it's a beacon signaling your commitment to academic excellence. Visualize it as a lighthouse guiding admissions officers through the stormy seas of applications. Maintaining a competitive GPA involves a strategic blend of diligence, focus, and resilience. Picture the satisfaction of seeing your GPA standing tall, a testament to your dedication.

Seeing the Bigger Picture: Course Selection Strategies

Selecting courses is akin to choosing the colors for your academic palette. Envision a canvas adorned with a rich array of challenging courses that showcase your intellectual curiosity and tenacity. It's not about collecting A's but demonstrating your willingness to embrace challenges. Picture the impact of a transcript adorned with courses that speak to your passion and determination.

Strategies for Success: Navigating Academic Challenges

Challenges are inevitable on this academic journey. Visualize them not as roadblocks but as stepping stones to growth. Whether it's a complex math problem, a demanding literature analysis, or a challenging science experiment, each hurdle is an opportunity to hone your skills. Picture the sense of accomplishment as you conquer academic challenges, emerging stronger and more capable.

The Support System: Nurturing Academic Growth

Even the most determined explorers have guides on their journeys. Picture your academic support system as the compass that keeps you on course. Seek mentors, teachers, or tutors who can provide guidance when the academic waters get choppy. Visualize the strength from knowing you're not alone – that support is readily available when needed.

The Power of Collaboration: Peer Support in Academics

Your fellow travelers in the academic realm are not competitors but companions on this journey. Envision the power of collaborative learning, where you exchange ideas, tackle challenges together, and celebrate shared successes. Picture the camaraderie of being part of a community that values academic growth and collective achievement.

Crafting Your Academic Story: Beyond Numbers and Grades

Your academic story is not confined to the numbers on your transcript; it's a narrative woven with experiences, lessons, and personal growth. Visualize your academic profile as a story that admissions officers eagerly delve into. It's not just about what you've learned in the classroom but how you've applied that knowledge to real-world challenges.

The Tapestry of Academic Growth: A Visual Feast for Admissions Officers

Imagine your academic profile as a tapestry, each thread representing a course, a grade, or a challenge conquered. Picture admissions officers marveling at this visual feast, captivated by the richness of your academic journey. It's not just about meeting expectations; it's about exceeding them and creating a narrative that leaves a lasting impression.

Embodying Your Academic Potential: A Visual Journey

As you delve into this chapter, visualize your academic potential not as an abstract concept but as a visual journey. See yourself excelling in challenging courses, overcoming obstacles, and embracing the support system that propels you forward. Picture your academic profile as a vibrant canvas reflecting your commitment to excellence.

Conclusion: A Strong Academic Profile Unveiled

In conclusion, this chapter guides you in crafting a strong academic profile – a vital component of your college admissions journey. It's not just about grades; it's about the resilience, challenges, and growth embedded in your academic narrative. As you navigate this odyssey, envision your GPA as a beacon, your course selection as a palette, and your academic story as a tapestry. Strengthen your academic profile, and let it stand as a testament to your commitment to excellence. The canvas is yours – paint it boldly.

.

STEP 3: NAVIGATING THE EXTRACURRICULAR LANDSCAPE

Extracurricular activities are checkboxes and windows into your character, leadership skills, and passions. You can discover strategically choosing and engaging in activities that align with your interests. Whether it's community service, sports, or clubs, this step guides you on leveraging extracurriculars to enhance your overall application.

Navigating the Extracurricular Landscape - Unveiling Your Character and Passions

Extracurricular activities are not mere checkboxes but the windows through which your character, leadership skills, and passions shine. This chapter delves into strategically choosing and engaging in activities that align with your interests. Whether it's community service, sports, or clubs, this step is your guide to leveraging extracurriculars enhancing the canvas of your overall application.

A Canvas Beyond Academics: The Essence of Extracurriculars

Imagine your college application as a canvas, painted with academic achievements and vibrant strokes of extracurricular involvement. Extracurriculars are the hues that add depth, showcasing facets of your character and passions beyond the classroom. Please visualize each activity as a brushstroke contributing to the masterpiece of your application.

Strategic Choices: Aligning Activities with Your Interests

Choosing extracurricular activities is not a random selection but a strategic decision. Picture yourself as an architect, carefully designing your involvement based on genuine interests. Envision activities that resonate with your passions, aligning perfectly with the narrative you'd like to present. See each choice as a deliberate step toward crafting a holistic and authentic profile.

Community Service: Impacting Lives, Shaping Character

Community service is not just a checkbox; it's a transformative journey. Picture yourself engaged in activities that contribute to the well-being of others. Feel the satisfaction of positively impacting lives, and visualize how these experiences shape your character. Extracurriculars become a channel for empathy, leadership, and a sense of responsibility.

Sports: Beyond the Field, Lessons for Life

Engaging in sports is more than a physical activity; it's a classroom for life lessons. Imagine yourself on the field or court, feeling the adrenaline, camaraderie, and joy of accomplishment. Visualize how these experiences cultivate teamwork, discipline, and resilience – qualities extending beyond sports, enriching your character.

Clubs and Organizations: Nurturing Interests, Fostering Connections

Clubs and organizations are not just meetings but spaces where shared passions come to life. Picture yourself actively participating in a club that aligns with your interests. Feel the sense of belonging, the exchange of ideas, and the connections forged. Extracurriculars become avenues for personal growth, leadership, and the joy of shared pursuits.

Leadership Roles: Guiding and Inspiring Others

Imagine stepping into a leadership role within an extracurricular activity. Feel the weight of responsibility, the thrill of guiding others, and the satisfaction of seeing a collective vision come to fruition. Visualize how these leadership experiences go beyond titles, showcasing your ability to inspire and lead – qualities that resonate with admissions officers.

Leveraging Extracurriculars: Enhancing Your Application Story

As you navigate the extracurricular landscape, envision the collective impact of your activities on your application story. See admissions officers immersing themselves in the narrative of your involvement – the genuine passions, the transformative experiences, and the character traits forged. Extracurriculars become the threads weaving a tapestry that goes beyond academics.

Conclusion: Extracurriculars as Catalysts for Growth

In conclusion, this chapter celebrates extracurriculars as catalysts for personal growth and character development. As you strategically choose and engage in activities, visualize the impact beyond the checkbox. See yourself as a multifaceted individual, enriched by experiences shaping your college application and journey toward success. Extracurriculars are not just additions but integral chapters in the compelling story of your academic and personal evolution. The canvas is yours – paint it with purpose.

STEP 4: MASTERING THE ART OF THE PERSONAL STATEMENT AND THE APPLICATION

Your personal statement is your chance to speak directly to admissions officers. Learn how to craft a compelling and authentic personal statement that reflects your journey, aspirations, and the impact you wish to make. This step provides practical tips, examples, and exercises to help you articulate your story with clarity and impact.

Crafting Your Compelling Personal Statement - Your Voice, Your Story

Your personal statement is not just a written piece; it's your direct conversation with admissions officers. In this chapter, you'll unravel the art of crafting a compelling and authentic personal statement that reflects your unique journey, aspirations, and the impact you wish to make. Practical tips, examples, and exercises await you, guiding you to articulate your story with clarity and impact.

Your Voice, Your Statement: A Direct Conversation

Envision your statement as a conversation – a direct exchange of thoughts and experiences between you and admissions officers. Picture your voice resonating through the words on the page, creating a connection that transcends the application process. Your statement becomes a narrative bridge, inviting admissions officers to enter your world.

Authenticity Unveiled: Crafting a Genuine Narrative

Authenticity is the heartbeat of your statement. Imagine the admissions officer reading your words and feeling the sincerity behind each sentence. Visualize the power of sharing your genuine experiences, aspirations, and perspectives. Your statement becomes a testament to your authenticity, a narrative that leaves a lasting impression.

Journey, Aspirations, Impact: The Three Pillars of Your Statement

Your statement revolves around your journey, aspirations, and the impact you aim to make. Picture these pillars as foundational elements, supporting a narrative that unfolds seamlessly. Your journey becomes a story, your aspirations a compass, and the impact you wish to make a guiding light. Visualize how these pillars converge to create a narrative of depth and purpose.

Practical Tips for Articulating Your Story: Exercises for Clarity

Crafting your statement is a process guided by helpful tips and exercises. Envision engaging in exercises that help clarify your narrative. See yourself refining your words, sharpening your focus, and articulating your story with precision. These exercises become tools, sculpting your statement into a piece that reflects your true essence.

Examples That Illuminate: Guiding Lights for Your Narrative

Examples serve as guiding lights, illuminating the path toward a compelling personal statement. Picture reading examples that resonate with your experiences, sparking ideas and inspiration. I'd like you to please show how these examples offer insights into structure, tone, and authenticity, empowering you to infuse your statement with a captivating allure.

Seeing, Feeling, Experiencing: Your Statement in Motion

As you delve into crafting your statement, imagine it in motion. Picture the admissions officer reading your words and being transported into your world. Feel the emotional impact of your narrative, envisioning the connection forged through your authentic voice. Your statement becomes dynamic, engaging, and resonating with those who read it.

Amplifying Emotional Impact: The Power of Your Personal Story

Amplify the emotional impact of your statement. Visualize admissions officers, not just reading but experiencing your story. Your words become a journey, evoking emotions and leaving an indelible mark. Picture the admissions officer connecting with your narrative personally, moved by the authenticity and power of your unique story.

A Mirror Reflecting You: Your Personal Statement Unveiled

As you conclude this chapter, see your personal statement as a mirror reflecting your essence. It's not just a document; it's a manifestation of your journey, aspirations, and the impact you wish to make. Envision admissions officers recognizing your voice's uniqueness and your narrative's authenticity. Your statement becomes a compelling testament to who you are and the contributions you bring.

Excerpt:

As I stand at the threshold of my college journey, I am propelled forward by a love for machines that intertwines with my fervor for mechanical engineering. From a young age, I found solace in the rhythmic hum of engines and the intricate dance of gears, igniting a curiosity that evolved into a fervent desire to explore the realms of mechanical systems. My journey into this field is not merely an academic pursuit but a personal odyssey fueled by a profound connection to the world of machinery.

Growing up in a small town, I discovered the beauty in the simplicity of mechanical marvels that surrounded our modest home. My fascination with the seamless integration of components and the sheer ingenuity behind every mechanism became the cornerstone of my journey. However, the path to pursuing mechanical engineering has been strewn with challenges. Being the first in my family to navigate the complexities of higher education, I faced uncertainties and doubts. Yet, it is precisely these hurdles that have fortified my resolve and sculpted my character.

In my high school years, I immersed myself in every available opportunity to deepen my understanding of mechanical systems. I sought mentorship from professionals who graciously shared their insights. These experiences expanded my knowledge and instilled in me the importance of innovation, precision, and collaboration in pursuing mechanical excellence.

Beyond the academic realm, I am driven by a commitment to applying mechanical engineering principles to address real-world challenges. Witnessing the transformative impact of efficient and sustainable technologies, I initiated projects that aimed to enhance energy efficiency and reduce environmental impact. The joy of seeing tangible results mirrored the transformative power of applying engineering prowess to create meaningful change.

In the halls of your esteemed institution, I see a bastion of academic excellence, a community that values innovation and creativity, and a crucible for forging lifelong connections. I am eager to contribute to this tapestry, bringing my passion for mechanical engineering, commitment to sustainable solutions, and a relentless pursuit of knowledge.

As I embark on this journey, I carry with me a thirst for academic prowess and a deep-rooted belief in the transformative power of engineering. My personal statement is not a mere admission requirement; it is an invitation to glimpse into the intricate world of machines that have shaped my experiences, aspirations, and the unwavering determination that propels me toward the forefront of mechanical innovation.

Remember, personal statements should be authentic reflections of the individual, showcasing their unique journey, aspirations, and what they can contribute to the college community. This is a general example; students should tailor their personal statements to reflect their experiences and goals.

Conclusion: Your Personal Statement, Your Legacy

In conclusion, this chapter celebrates the journey of crafting your statement – a piece that encapsulates your voice, story, and legacy. As you envision the admissions officer reading your words, feel the power of your narrative, leaving an indelible impression. Your statement reflects your authenticity, purpose, and the impact you aspire to make. The pen is in your hand – let your voice resonate.

Completing The Application:

Embarking on the final stretch of your college application journey is like stepping onto a stage where your unique story takes center stage. This phase is all about you – your passions, challenges, and triumphs coming together to form a narrative that will captivate those making the admissions decisions.

As you navigate the completion of your college application, it's not just about ticking off boxes; it's about painting a vivid portrait of who you are. Imagine this as the moment you showcase your character, ambitions, and the essence of what makes you, well, you.

The College Application will include requests for the following:

Personal Information:
- Full Name
- Date of Birth
- Gender
- Mailing Address
- Email Address
- Phone Number

Academic Information:
- High School Name, Address, and Graduation Date
- GPA (weighted and unweighted)
- Class Rank (if available)
- List of Courses and Grades
- Standardized Test Scores (SAT, ACT)

Extracurricular Activities:
- Clubs and Organizations
- Sports and Athletic Achievements
- Community Service and Volunteer Work
- Leadership Roles
- Part-time Jobs or Internships

Awards and Honors:
- Academic Achievements
- Recognitions or Certificates
- Scholarships or Grants Received

Essays:
- Personal Statement: A narrative about your background, experiences, and goals.
- Supplemental Essays: Responses to specific prompts provided by the college.

Recommendation Letters:
- Letters from teachers, counselors, or other mentors who can speak to your character, achievements, and potential. Be sure to provide a brag sheet when you email your request. This provides important information that you want included in your letter.

Portfolio (if applicable):
- Art, Writing, or Performance portfolios may be required for certain programs.

Interviews (if applicable):
- Some colleges may require or offer optional interviews to learn more about applicants.

Financial Aid Information:
- FAFSA (Free Application for Federal Student Aid) or other financial aid application details.
- Information about scholarships or grants you're applying for.

Parent/Guardian Information:
- Names and Occupations of Parents/Guardians
- Household Income Information

Transcripts and Test Scores:
- Submit official high school transcripts.
- Arrange for standardized test scores to be sent directly to the college.

Remember, the specifics can vary, so it's crucial to carefully read and follow the instructions on each college's application form. Pay attention to deadlines and provide accurate and honest information. Tailor your essays to showcase your personality and unique qualities, and use your application as an opportunity to present yourself holistically to the admissions committee.

Brag Sheet for Letter of Recommendation:

Dear [Teacher's Name],

I would appreciate your support in writing a letter of recommendation for my college applications. I greatly value your insights into my character, work ethic, and achievements. Your support means a lot to me, and your perspective will provide colleges with a comprehensive understanding of my abilities.

Personal Information:
- Full Name: [Your Full Name]
- Current Grade: [Grade]
- Contact Information: [Email and Phone Number]

Academic Achievements:
- GPA: [Current GPA]
- Relevant Courses: [List any advanced or honors courses]
- Academic Awards/Honors: [Any awards or honors received]

Extracurricular Activities:
- Clubs/Organizations: [List clubs or organizations you're involved in]
- Leadership Positions: [Specify any leadership roles held]
- Community Service: [Describe your involvement in community service]
- Sports/Arts: [If applicable, mention your participation in sports or arts]

Work Experience/Internships:
- Part-Time Jobs: [Specify any part-time jobs you've held]
- Internships/Volunteer Work: [Describe relevant internships or volunteer experiences]

Special Skills or Talents:
- Languages: [If proficient in any languages]
- Technical Skills: [Specify any technical skills or certifications]
- Other Talents: [Mention any unique talents or skills]

Achievements Outside the Classroom:
- Competitions: [Specify any competitions or contests you've participated in]
- Projects: [Highlight any significant projects you've worked on]
  - Published Work: [If applicable, mention any published articles, essays, etc.]

Goals and Aspirations:
- College and Career Goals: [Outline your academic and career aspirations]
- How [College Name] Fits Your Goals: [Explain why you're interested in attending the specific college]

Challenges and Growth:
- Overcoming Challenges: [Share any challenges you've faced and overcome]
- Personal Growth: [Describe how you've grown and developed during high school]

Additional Information:
- Any Additional Information: [Include any information you think is relevant for the recommendation]

Conclusion: I appreciate your time and consideration in writing this letter. Your insights will provide colleges with a well-rounded view of who I am. If you have any questions or need more information, please feel free to contact me. Thank you for being so supportive.

Sincerely, [Your Full Name]
[Your Contact Information]

Complete the following brag sheet and attach it to the email that you send to your instructors.

Sample Letter of Recommendation Email

Dear [Teacher's Name],

I would appreciate your support in writing a letter of recommendation for my college applications. I greatly value your insights into my character, work ethic, and achievements. Your support means a lot to me, and your perspective will provide colleges with a comprehensive understanding of my abilities.

I appreciate your time and consideration in writing this letter. Your insights will provide colleges with a well-rounded view of who I am. I have attached my brag sheet with this email. If you have any questions or need more information, please feel free to contact me. Thank you for being so supportive.

Sincerely,

[Your Full Name]
[Your Contact Information]

Senior Brag Sheet

Name _____ Address _____
Phone Number _____ Email _____

Academics:

GPA _____ Credits Completed _____ Desired Major _____

Academic Award/Honor	Description	Years Received
		9 10 11 12
		9 10 11 12
		9 10 11 12
		9 10 11 12
		9 10 11 12
		9 10 11 12

Extracurricular and Community:

Specify what activities, events, sports, and work you have participated in outside classes.

Organization or Event	Years of Involvement	Activity or Position Held	Hours of Service or Participation
	9 10 11 12		
	9 10 11 12		
	9 10 11 12		
	9 10 11 12		
	9 10 11 12		
	9 10 11 12		
	9 10 11 12		

STEP 5: ACING INTERVIEWS AND CAMPUS VISITS

The interview stage is an opportunity to showcase your personality and demonstrate why you're a perfect fit for the college. From preparing for common questions to mastering the art of first impressions, this step equips you with the skills and confidence needed to shine during interviews and campus visits.

Acing Interviews and Campus Visits - Your Moment to Shine

The interview stage is not just a conversation; it's your opportunity to showcase your personality and prove why you're the perfect fit for the college. From preparing for common questions to mastering the art of first impressions, this step equips you with the skills and confidence needed to shine during interviews and campus visits.

Setting the Stage: The Importance of Interviews and Campus Visits

Picture the interview and campus visit as the stage where you step into the spotlight. Imagine the admissions officer is eager to meet the person behind the application. See the campus as the canvas where your journey could unfold. Feel the anticipation, knowing this is your moment to make a lasting impression.

Preparing for Success: Anticipating Common Questions

Imagine yourself preparing for the interview, anticipating the questions that might come your way. Envision practicing your responses with confidence and clarity. Picture the interview room as a space where your experiences, aspirations, and personality will come to life. Knowing you're well-prepared to navigate the conversation, visualize the sense of readiness.

Mastering First Impressions: The Art of Authenticity

First impressions matter, and mastering them is an art. Picture yourself walking onto the campus, feeling a sense of belonging. Envision the admissions officer greeted by your authentic self during the interview. See the positive impact of genuine smiles, firm handshakes, and eye contact. The art of authenticity becomes your secret weapon in leaving a lasting impression.

Connecting Through Stories: Weaving Narratives in Interviews

Stories have the power to connect. Imagine weaving narratives during the interview, sharing experiences that illustrate your character and values. Visualize the admissions officer engaged, captivated by the stories that reveal the essence of who you are. Feel

the connection deepen as your narratives unfold,
making you memorable in the eyes of the interviewer.

Navigating Campus Visits: Seeing Your Future Home

As you step onto the campus, envision it as your future home. Feel the environment's energy, see yourself exploring the facilities, and imagine the interactions with students and faculty.

You can visualize the connection as if the campus is welcoming you into its community. The campus visit becomes a glimpse into your next chapter.

Building Confidence: Embracing Your Unique Qualities

Confidence is your ally during interviews and campus visits. Imagine embracing your unique qualities, knowing you bring something distinctive to the college community. Visualize the admissions officer recognizing your strengths and the value you would add. Feel the confidence emanating from your genuine self-expression.

Handling Challenges: Turning Moments Into Opportunities

Challenges may arise during interviews or campus visits. Envision yourself in handling these moments with grace and resilience. See challenges as opportunities to showcase your adaptability and problem-solving skills. Visualize the admissions officer acknowledging your ability to navigate unforeseen circumstances, leaving a positive impression.

Leaving a Lasting Impression: The Aftermath of Your Presence

As the interview ends and the campus visit ends, I'd like you to imagine the aftermath of your presence. Picture the admissions officer reflecting on the conversation, recalling your authentic stories. Imagine the campus remembering your footsteps as if already anticipating your return. Your presence leaves a lasting impression, imprinting your candidacy in their memory.

Embracing the Journey: The Final Steps Toward Acceptance

In conclusion, the interview and campus visit are integral steps toward acceptance. Visualize the journey you've embarked on – from preparing for questions to mastering first impressions. Feel the sense of accomplishment, knowing you've showcased your unique qualities authentically. The interview and campus visit become chapters in your success story, bringing you closer to the bright future that awaits you.

Conclusion: Your Presence, Your Potential

In conclusion, this chapter celebrates your presence as the key to unlocking your potential. As you navigate interviews and campus visits, envision the doors of opportunity swinging open. Feel the excitement of knowing your authentic self has left an indelible mark. Your presence becomes the catalyst for acceptance, and the journey continues with newfound confidence and anticipation.

Acing a college interview and campus visit involves careful preparation and a genuine expression of interest. Here are some tips for students:

- **Research the College:**
  - Familiarize yourself with the college's history, values, and academic programs.
  - Explore specific departments or majors you are interested in.
- **Prepare for Common Questions:**
  - Anticipate common interview questions and formulate thoughtful responses.
  - Be ready to discuss your academic interests, extracurricular activities, and career aspirations.
- **Ask Informed Questions:**
  - Prepare questions that demonstrate your genuine interest in the college.
  - Inquire about specific programs, research opportunities, or unique aspects of campus life.
- **Dress Appropriately:**
  - Choose attire that reflects professionalism and respect for the occasion.
  - Dressing well contributes to a positive first impression.
- **Express Enthusiasm:**
  - Demonstrate your enthusiasm for the college and its offerings.
  - Express how you see yourself contributing to the campus community.
- **Bring a Notepad:**
  - Bring a notepad and pen to jot down important information or insights during the visit.
  - This shows that you are attentive and value the information shared.

7. Follow Up with Gratitude:

- Send a thank-you email expressing your appreciation for the interview and campus visit.
- Reiterate your interest in the college and highlight any specific aspects that resonated with you.

Both administrators and students play pivotal roles in creating a positive and informative experience during college interviews and campus visits. It's a collaborative effort to ensure that prospective students gain valuable insights into the college's offerings and feel welcomed into the community.

STEP 6: NAVIGATING FINANCIAL AID AND SCHOLARSHIPS

Financial considerations should not hinder your pursuit of higher education. This step guides you through the intricacies of navigating financial aid and scholarships. Learn how to research and apply for financial assistance, ensuring that your dream college remains an attainable goal.

Navigating Financial Aid and Scholarships - Empowering Your Educational Journey

Financial considerations should never stand as barriers to your pursuit of higher education. This step guides you through the intricacies of navigating financial aid and scholarships. By understanding how to research and apply for financial assistance, you ensure that your dream college remains an attainable goal.

Painting a Picture of Financial Freedom

Envision financial freedom as a landscape where your educational dreams can thrive. Picture yourself standing at the intersection of possibilities, with pathways leading to your desired college. Feel the weight lifted off your shoulders, knowing that financial aid and scholarships are the keys to unlocking these pathways.

Demystifying Financial Aid: Your Beacon in the Darkness

Financial aid might seem like an intricate maze, but imagine it as a guiding light illuminating your way. See yourself confidently navigating the process, understanding the types of aid available. Visualize financial assistance as a beacon in the darkness, dispelling uncertainties and ensuring your educational journey remains well-lit.

Exploring Scholarships: Your Personal Treasures

Think of scholarships as treasures waiting to be discovered on your educational journey. Picture yourself exploring these opportunities, each scholarship shining as a valuable gem. Imagine the pride and excitement as you uncover scholarships aligned with your aspirations. Scholarships become the means to enrich your educational experience.

Researching Financial Assistance: Your Personal Expedition

Envision researching financial assistance as a personal expedition to get your educational future. See yourself equipped with the tools and knowledge needed to explore available options. Feel the satisfaction of uncovering resources tailored to your needs. The research process becomes an empowering expedition, ensuring financial barriers are dismantled.

Applying for Aid: Your Proactive Step Towards Success

Applying for financial aid is not a hurdle but a proactive step toward success. Picture yourself completing applications with ease, armed with a sense of purpose and determination. Envision the opening doors of opportunity as your applications are received and processed. Applying for aid becomes a strategic move in your journey.

Celebrating Success: The Fruits of Your Financial Planning

As financial aid and scholarship offers come in, imagine the sense of accomplishment and relief. Visualize the doors of your dream college swinging open, each offer representing a triumph over financial obstacles. Feel the joy of knowing that your commitment to financial planning has borne fruit. Success becomes a celebration of resilience and determination.

Creating Financial Stability: Your Foundation for Success

Financial stability is the foundation upon which your educational success rests. Envision yourself building this foundation, each opportunity of financial assistance and scholarship contributing to its strength. Picture the sense of security knowing that your dream college is not just a vision but a tangible goal. Financial stability becomes the bedrock of your educational journey.

Inspiring Others: The Ripple Effect of Financial Empowerment

Imagine the ripple effect of financial empowerment extending beyond yourself—picture future generations inspired by your journey, confidently breaking through financial barriers. Envision a community where education is a beacon of hope and your story catalyzes change. Your financial empowerment becomes a source of inspiration for others.

When applying for a scholarship, students should include the following:

- Academic Achievements: Highlight your academic accomplishments, including GPA, class rank, and any honors or awards received.
- Extracurricular Activities: Showcase your involvement in clubs, sports, community service, or other extracurriculars to demonstrate leadership, teamwork, and time management skills.
- Volunteer Experience: Emphasize any volunteer work or community service, emphasizing the impact it has had on both you and the community.
- Work Experience: Include relevant work experience, internships, or part-time jobs, emphasizing skills gained and lessons learned.
- Letters of Recommendation: Attach letters of recommendation from teachers, mentors, or employers who can speak to your character and abilities.

- Personal Statement or Essay: Write a compelling essay that shares your story, goals, and why you deserve the scholarship. Be authentic and passionate.
- Financial Need Statement: If applicable, provide a clear and honest statement about your financial situation, detailing why the scholarship would make a significant impact.
- Transcripts: Include official transcripts to validate your academic achievements.

Each scholarship may have specific requirements, so tailor your application accordingly. Always follow application instructions closely and submit a polished, well-organized application to stand out.

Conclusion: Your Financial Journey, Your Educational Triumph

In conclusion, see your financial journey as integral to your educational triumph. Visualize the open doors of opportunity fueled by financial aid and scholarships. Feel the empowerment of knowing that financial barriers are not roadblocks but stepping stones toward your dream college. Your financial journey becomes a testament to resilience, determination, and the limitless potential within you.

Scholarships are a doorway to turning dreams into reality. As you navigate this landscape, envision it as a treasure hunt, with each essay as your map leading to golden opportunities. Now, let's delve into the heart of scholarship applications and uncover the secrets to making your essays shine. Per TheFinlitguy on Instagram, you can use the following five types of essays for most of your scholarship application essay writing.

Think of the Rags to Riches essay as your hero's journey. Share the challenges you've faced, the obstacles you've overcome – your personal odyssey. Make the reader feel the struggle and triumph; let them see the underdog rising to conquer the odds.

Shift gears to the Your Impact on the World essay. Paint a vivid picture of the positive change you aspire to bring. Whether it's in your community, globally, or within your chosen field, make the reader visualize the ripple effect of your contributions.

In the "What Will You Do with the Money" essay, go beyond discussing goals; vividly depict your aspirations. Illustrate how scholarship funds will impact your journey, covering tuition or supporting transformative projects. Take the reader on a guided tour of your future, describing how the scholarship empowers you to seize opportunities and break barriers. Convey the tangible impact on your educational pursuits, making it easy for the reader to envision the transformative effect. Infuse your plans with passion, allowing the reader to sense your excitement and dedication, turning this opportunity into a springboard for future success.

Next up, the What Field of Study essay – your chance to showcase your academic aspirations. Bring your chosen field to life; make it tangible and exciting. Help the reader see the passion and curiosity that fuels your desire to dive deep into this realm.

The Wild Card essay is your canvas to paint with the colors of current events. Dive into the world around you – the challenges, triumphs, and transformations. Make it relevant, make it impactful, and most importantly, make it uniquely yours.

Imagine these essays as threads weaving a tapestry of your character, dreams, and potential. Each essay is a stroke of the brush, contributing to the masterpiece that is your scholarship application. The goal is not just to impress but to connect – to make the reader feel your journey, your impact, and your dreams.

So, dive in with the spirit of an adventurer seeking treasures. Craft your essays with passion, honesty, and a touch of flair that makes them memorable. Let your words be the beacon that guides scholarship committees to recognize the gem that you are.

Ready to embark on this thrilling journey? Let the scholarship essays be your compass, guiding you toward a future bright with possibilities.

STEP 7: CRAFTING A STELLAR RESUME

Your resume is a snapshot of your achievements and experiences. This step breaks down the elements of a stellar resume, guiding you on effectively highlight your accomplishments. A well-crafted resume can be a powerful tool in showcasing your capabilities to admissions officers.

Crafting a Stellar Resume - Your Gateway to Recognition

Your resume is more than a document; it's a snapshot of your achievements and experiences—a key to unlocking the door of recognition. This step breaks down the elements of a stellar resume, guiding you on effectively highlight your accomplishments. Picture your resume as a powerful tool, showcasing your capabilities to admissions officers and leaving an indelible mark.

A Glimpse Into Your Achievements

Imagine your resume as a gallery showcasing your most prized achievements. Picture each accomplishment as a masterpiece, framed and ready for admiration. Feel the pride and confidence emanating from your resume, telling a story of your journey, passions, and successes.

Painting a Vivid Picture

Your resume is not just words on paper; it's a canvas where you paint a vivid picture of your capabilities. Envision each section as brush strokes, contributing to the overall masterpiece. Feel the colors of your experiences coming to life, creating a visually appealing and compelling narrative.

Showcasing Your Leadership Journey

See your leadership experiences showcased prominently on your resume. Imagine admissions officers recognizing your ability to lead, inspire, and make a positive impact. Visualize your leadership roles as shining beacons, guiding the reader through your growth and influence narrative.

Highlighting Your Character and Values

Your resume is a reflection of your character and values. Picture the values you hold dear reflected in every line, creating a portrait of integrity, resilience, and compassion. Feel the connection between your experiences and the values that define you, leaving a lasting impression on those who read your resume.

Crafting Impactful Descriptions

Envision your resume filled with impactful descriptions that resonate with the reader. Picture each word as a brushstroke, contributing to the overall

Turning Challenges Into Triumphs

See your resume as a testament to overcoming challenges. Visualize admissions officers recognizing your ability to turn obstacles into triumphs. Imagine your journey portrayed as a narrative of resilience, determination, and growth. Your challenges become stepping stones to success, evident in every section of your resume.

Creating a Lasting Impression

Picture your resume leaving a lasting impression on admissions officers. Envision them reading through your accomplishments with admiration and intrigue. Feel the impact of your resume resonating with the reader, creating a sense of anticipation to learn more about the individual behind the document.

Empowering Your Application

Your well-crafted resume becomes a powerful tool, empowering your college application. Imagine it as the key that unlocks doors of opportunity. Visualize admissions officers recognizing your unique strengths and contributions, eager to welcome you into their academic community.

Conclusion: Your Resume, Your Story

In conclusion, your resume is not just a collection of details; it's your story told through achievements, experiences, and values. Picture it as a dynamic narrative that sets you apart. Feel the confidence from crafting a stellar resume, knowing your story is ready to be shared with the world. Your resume becomes a gateway to recognition, paving your journey to higher education.

Sample Resume

[Your Name]
[Your Address]
[City, State ZIP Code]
[Your Email Address]
[Your Phone Number]

Objective: Aspiring college student seeking admission to [College/University] with a passion for [your intended major]. Eager to contribute academic achievements, leadership skills, and extracurricular experiences to the campus community.

Education:
- High School Diploma [High School Name, City, State] Graduation Date: [Month, Year] GPA: [Your GPA]

Academic Achievements:
- [Any honors, awards, or recognition received during high school]

Extracurricular Activities:
- President, [High School Club/Organization] [Brief description of your role and achievements]

- Varsity [Sport] Team Member [Details about your involvement, achievements, and leadership roles]
- Volunteer, [Community Service Organization] [Description of volunteer work and impact]

Work Experience:
- Sales Associate, [Retail Store] [Month, Year - Month, Year] [Brief description of responsibilities and accomplishments]
- Intern, [Company] [Month, Year - Month, Year] [Summary of internship role and contributions]

Skills:
- [List any relevant skills such as languages, computer programs, or certifications]

References:
Available upon request.

Remember to tailor your resume to highlight your unique strengths and experiences. Include quantifiable achievements whenever possible, and keep the content concise and focused on what's most relevant to your college application.

Ben Smith

555-584-9555
bensmith@email.com
Anywhere, GA 12345

OBJECTIVE

Aspiring college student seeking admission to [College/University] with a passion for [your intended major]. Eager to contribute academic achievements, leadership skills, and extracurricular experiences to the campus community.

EDUCATION

Anywhere High School, Anywhere, Georgia
4.0 GPA
2024 graduation

Relevant skills

- Punctual
- Strong communication skills
- Excellent in mathematics
- Proficient in French and English
- Great interpersonal skills

WORK EXPERIENCE

Volunteer
A Bright Star Rescue, January 2023–December 2023

- Play with dogs and cats regularly so they don't get lonely
- Restock shelves with food and supplies
- Greet people coming in and introduce them to the animals

Volunteer
Anywhere Shelter, June 2021–January 2023

- Served meals and drinks to anyone who entered
- Swept and mopped the floors at the end of the day
- Helped prepare meals

Academic Achievements

- Honor roll in grades 9, 10, 11 and 12
- Recognition for having the highest grade in mathematics throughout high school
- Perfect attendance award in grades 11 and 12

STEP 8: BUILDING AN ONLINE PRESENCE

In today's digital age, an online presence is increasingly significant. Discover how to curate a professional online persona that complements your college application. This step provides insights into leveraging platforms like LinkedIn and creating a digital footprint that reflects your academic and extracurricular achievements.

Building an Online Presence - Crafting Your Digital Identity

In today's digital landscape, your online presence is more than a virtual snapshot; it's a dynamic reflection of your accomplishments and aspirations. This step unveils the secrets to curating a professional online persona that seamlessly aligns with your college application. Picture yourself navigating the digital realm, strategically leveraging platforms like LinkedIn, and leaving a lasting impression with a digital footprint that showcases your academic and extracurricular achievements.

Navigating the Digital Landscape

Envision the digital landscape as a vast canvas where your online presence takes center stage. Picture yourself confidently navigating this space, each click contributes to the masterpiece of your digital identity. Feel the excitement as you embark on a journey to curate an online persona that complements your academic journey.

Curating a Professional Persona

See yourself crafting a professional online persona that reflects your unique qualities. Imagine admissions officers encountering your digital identity and gaining insights into your character, leadership skills, and passions. Visualize your digital presence as a mirror reflecting the best aspects of your academic and extracurricular achievements.

Leveraging the Power of LinkedIn

Envision the power of LinkedIn as a tool to amplify your professional image. Picture yourself optimizing your profile and strategically connecting with influencers in your interest. Feel the impact of your LinkedIn presence, creating a digital narrative that resonates with admissions officers and peers alike.

Creating a Digital Footprint of Achievements

See your digital footprint becoming a testament to your academic and extracurricular successes. Visualize a trail of achievements, each leaving an indelible mark on the digital landscape. Imagine admissions officers following this trail, gaining a deeper understanding of your journey and impact in various spheres.

Making Every Click Count

Picture every click, post, and interaction contributing to the narrative of your digital identity. Envision each online activity as a brushstroke, adding layers of depth and authenticity to your virtual presence. Feel the sense of purpose as you make every click count, creating a digital story that resonates with your academic ambitions.

Crafting a Digital Narrative of Excellence

Imagine your digital narrative unfolding like a captivating story of excellence. Visualize admissions officers reading your online profile with intrigue and admiration. Feel the power of a well-crafted digital identity seamlessly woven into the fabric of your college application, enhancing the overall impact and resonance.

Embracing the Future

See yourself embracing the future with a powerful online presence. Picture the doors of opportunity opening due to your strategic and authentic digital identity. Visualize your online presence as a reflection and a catalyst for your academic and professional journey, setting the stage for success.

Here are some strategies for students on what to do and include in their social online profiles:

For Students:

- **Create a Social Media Profile:**
  - Develop a professional profile highlighting academic achievements, extracurricular activities, and career goals.
  - Connect with current students, alumni, and college administrators.
- **Showcase Achievements:**
  - Share academic achievements, awards, and participation in extracurricular activities on social media platforms.
  - Use visuals such as images or videos to enhance engagement.
- **Engage in Online Communities:**
  - Participate in online communities related to the college or specific academic interests.
  - Contribute to discussions and connect with peers and administrators.
- **Attend Virtual College Fairs:**
  - Attend virtual college fairs and engage with college representatives.
  - Ask questions and express your interest in the college.
- **Connect with College Social Media:**
  - Follow the college's official social media accounts to stay updated on events, news, and important announcements.
  - Engage with posts and share content that resonates with you.
  - Use hashtags related to the college to increase visibility.

Conclusion: Your Digital Identity, Your Legacy

In conclusion, your digital identity is not just a collection of online activities; it's a legacy in the making. Picture it as a testament to your achievements, ambitions, and the impact you wish to make. Feel the confidence from crafting a digital persona aligned with your aspirations. Your online presence becomes a powerful asset, propelling you into a future where every click contributes to your success.

STEP 9: NAVIGATING WAITLISTS AND DEFERRALS

What if you find yourself on a waitlist or face a deferral? This step offers strategies and insights on navigating these situations. Learn how to express continued interest, provide updates, and increase your chances of securing a spot.

Navigating Waitlists and Deferrals - Turning Uncertainty into Opportunity

Imagine facing the unexpected situation of finding yourself on a college waitlist or experiencing a deferral. This step guides you in transforming these moments of uncertainty into opportunities for success. You can picture yourself navigating the complexities with strategies that show continued interest, provide updates, and greatly increase your chances of securing that spot.

The Unexpected Twist: Waitlists and Deferrals

Picture the moment when you receive unexpected news—your application is on a waitlist or deferred. Feel the uncertainty and the surge of emotions that accompany this unexpected twist. This step is your compass, guiding you through the uncharted territory of waitlists and deferrals, turning these challenges into opportunities.

Strategies for Expressing Continued Interest

See yourself implementing strategies to express your continued interest in the college. Visualize crafting a compelling message that conveys your passion for the institution and showcases your resilience and determination. Feel the confidence that comes with navigating these situations with purpose and clarity.

Providing Meaningful Updates

Imagine the power of providing meaningful updates to the college. Visualize the impact of sharing significant achievements, personal growth, or new insights gained since your initial application. Picture the admissions officers recognizing your commitment to excellence and your ongoing pursuit of self-improvement.

Increasing Your Chances of Securing a Spot

Envision yourself strategically increasing your chances of securing a spot. See the effectiveness of your actions reflected in a renewed interest from the college. Feel the excitement as you navigate this process with skill and finesse, transforming a momentary setback into a stepping stone toward success.

Overcoming Uncertainty with Confidence

Picture yourself overcoming uncertainty with unwavering confidence. Visualize each step you take as a deliberate move toward securing your place. Feel the empowerment that comes from turning a challenging situation into an opportunity to demonstrate your dedication and resilience.

A Transformative Journey Towards Success

See this chapter as a transformative journey towards success, gracefully and with determination, navigating the twists and turns of waitlists and deferrals. Picture the result—a secured spot at the college of your dreams. Feel the sense of accomplishment as you reflect on your ability to turn uncertainty into an opportunity for growth and achievement.

Conclusion: From Waitlists to Triumphs

In conclusion, the journey from waitlists to triumphs is a testament to your resilience and strategic approach. Imagine the sense of triumph as you secure your place at the college. Picture the doors of opportunity swinging wide open, welcoming you into a future enriched by the challenges you've navigated with skill and determination. Your ability to turn uncertainty into triumphs becomes a defining chapter in your academic journey.

STEP 10: MAKING THE FINAL DECISION

Congratulations, you've been accepted to multiple colleges! Now comes the final decision-making process. This step helps you weigh financial aid, campus culture, and academic offerings to make an informed decision that aligns with your goals and aspirations.

Making the Final Decision - Your Path to a Bright Future

Congratulations! You've received acceptance letters from multiple colleges, and now it's time for the crucial final decision-making process. This step is your compass, guiding you through a thoughtful evaluation of factors like financial aid, campus culture, and academic offerings. It empowers you to make an informed decision that aligns seamlessly with your goals and aspirations, paving the way for a future filled with success and fulfillment.

A Moment of Celebration and Reflection

Picture the moment when you receive those coveted acceptance letters. Feel the joy, pride, and sense of accomplishment that comes with this significant achievement. This step is designed to help you savor this moment of celebration while preparing for the equally important decision-making journey ahead.

Weighing Financial Aid Options

Visualize yourself delving into the financial aid details offered by each college. See the importance of understanding the terms, scholarships, and grants available. This step guides you through a process where you can envision the financial aspects of your education, making a decision that aligns with your financial goals.

Immersing Yourself in Campus Culture

Imagine immersing yourself in the vibrant campus culture of each college. Picture the atmosphere, the community, and the opportunities that await. This step lets you feel each campus's pulse, ensuring that your chosen college supports your academic aspirations and resonates with your values and interests.

Exploring Academic Offerings

See yourself exploring the diverse academic offerings each college presents. Visualize the courses, programs, and faculty shaping your educational journey. This step empowers you to align with your academic goals, ensuring your college experience is transformative and tailored to your unique aspirations.

The Power of Informed Decision-Making

Feel the empowerment that comes with making an informed decision. Picture yourself confidently selecting the college that best aligns with your financial considerations, campus culture preferences, and academic aspirations. This step is more than choosing a college; it's about choosing the path leading to your future success.

Sealing Your Decision with Confidence

Envision the moment when you seal your decision with confidence. Feel the certainty in your choice, knowing it's grounded in a thoughtful evaluation of the factors that matter most to you. This step guides you towards a decision that opens the door to your academic journey and sets the stage for a future filled with achievements and personal growth.

Here is some advice for students making their final decision on college destination:

For Students:

- **Compare Financial Aid Packages:**
  - Compare and carefully analyze financial aid packages from each college.
  - Consider the overall cost of attendance, including tuition, fees, and living expenses.
- **Visit Campuses (Virtual or In-Person):**
  - Attend virtual or in-person campus visits to get a feel for the environment.
  - Explore academic facilities, dormitories, and recreational areas.

- **Talk to Current Students:**
  - Connect with current students through social media or official college forums.
  - Seek their perspectives on academics, social life, and campus culture.
- **Evaluate Academic Programs:**
  - Review the academic programs offered by each college and consider which aligns best with your career goals.
  - Explore internship and research opportunities within your field of study.
- **Consider Location and Campus Life:**
  - Evaluate the location of each college, considering factors such as climate, proximity to home, and available extracurricular activities.
  - Think about the type of campus environment that suits your preferences.
- **Consult with Mentors and Advisors:**
  - Seek advice from mentors, teachers, or high school advisors who can provide guidance based on your academic strengths and goals.
  - Discuss your options with individuals who know you well.
- **Reflect on Personal Goals:**
  - Reflect on your personal and academic goals, considering which college aligns with your aspirations.
  - Evaluate the resources and support services that will contribute to your success.

Both college administrators and students play essential roles in the decision-making process. By fostering open communication, providing comprehensive information, and creating opportunities for engagement, the final decision becomes a well-informed and mutually beneficial choice.

Conclusion: Embracing the Journey Ahead

In conclusion, making the final decision is a monumental step towards embracing the journey ahead. Picture the doors of opportunity swinging wide open as you embark on a path that aligns seamlessly with your goals and aspirations. Feel the excitement as you take charge of your future, confident in your decision. Your academic adventure awaits, and this step is your key to unlocking a future filled with success and fulfillment.

Tips From Experience

It's essential to keep all these documents organized and secure, as they will be valuable throughout your college acceptance journey and during your time in college. Digital backups and secure cloud storage options can help ensure that you don't lose important information. Here are some other important pieces of information and documents to save:

1. **Resume**:
   - **Purpose**: A resume is a concise document that summarizes a student's academic achievements, extracurricular activities, skills, and work experience.
   - **Why Save It**: Having a resume saved allows quick customization and submission for various applications. It's a dynamic document that should be updated regularly as the student achieves new milestones or gains more experience.
2. **Cover Letter**:
   - **Purpose**: A cover letter is a personalized letter to college admissions committees or scholarship boards that highlights a student's interest, qualifications, and reasons for applying.
   - **Why Save It**: Keeping a cover letter template can help in drafting tailored letters for different applications. It serves as a basis to highlight how a student's goals and values align with each college or scholarship.
3. **Transcript**:
   - **Purpose**: A transcript is an official record of a student's academic performance, including courses taken and grades received.
   - **Why Save It**: Colleges and scholarship committees require transcripts to assess academic readiness and performance. Having a digital copy ensures that it can be easily submitted when requested.

4. **Scholarship Essays**:
   - **Purpose**: Scholarship essays are written responses to prompts provided by scholarship organizations, showcasing a student's qualifications, experiences, and aspirations.
   - **Why Save It**: Scholarship essays can often be repurposed or adapted for different applications. Keeping them saved allows students to refer back to previous responses for inspiration or reuse.
5. **Letters of Recommendation**:
   - **Purpose**: These are letters from teachers, counselors, or mentors that endorse a student's abilities, character, and achievements.
   - **Why Save It**: While students typically don't submit recommendation letters themselves (as they are often sent directly to colleges or scholarship committees), having a copy can be helpful for reference or in cases where a recommender might need to resend it.
6. **Spreadsheet of Colleges Applied To**:
   - **Purpose**: This is a detailed list of colleges to which the student has applied, including relevant deadlines, requirements, and application statuses.
   - **Why Save It**: Keeping a spreadsheet helps track applications and stay organized. It ensures that the student meets all deadlines and completes all necessary steps for each college application.
7. **Spreadsheet of Scholarships Applied To**:
   - **Purpose**: Similar to the college spreadsheet, this tracks scholarship applications, including submission dates, requirements, and the status of each application.
   - **Why Save It**: It's crucial for managing multiple scholarship applications, tracking deadlines, and follow-ups. This organization helps maximize the chances of securing financial aid.

8. **Standardized Test Scores:**
   - **Purpose:** Standardized test scores (SAT, ACT, TOEFL, etc.) are often required for college applications and can be crucial for placement in certain courses or programs.
   - **Why Save It:** Keep copies for reference in case of discrepancies or if additional submissions are necessary. They may also be required for scholarship applications.
9. **Application Confirmation Emails:**
   - **Purpose:** These emails confirm the submission of your college applications and often contain important details like application IDs or reference numbers.
   - **Why Save It:** Useful for tracking your applications, following up with colleges, and verifying that your applications have been received.
10. **Financial Aid Information:**
    - **Purpose:** Documents related to financial aid, including the FAFSA and CSS Profile, are essential for determining eligibility for federal, state, and institutional aid.
    - **Why Save It:** Keeping these documents helps track what financial aid you've applied for and received and is useful for future reference or if any disputes arise.
11. **Admission Interview Notes:**
    - **Purpose:** Notes from admission interviews can provide valuable insights and reminders about what was discussed.
    - **Why Save It:** They can be useful for writing personalized thank-you notes, which can positively impact your application. They may also be helpful for future interviews or preparations.

12. **Portfolio or Audition Materials:**
    - **Purpose:** For programs in the arts, music, or performing arts, portfolios or audition materials showcase your skills and talents.
    - **Why Save It:** Useful for reapplication, other applications, or as a record of your work at the time of your college application.
13. **Admissions Communication:**
    - **Purpose:** Emails or letters from colleges can contain crucial information about admission decisions, deadlines, and additional requirements.
    - **Why Save It:** To ensure you have all the necessary information for each college and to track and comply with all requirements and deadlines.
14. **Scholarship Acceptance Letters:**
    - **Purpose:** These letters confirm your receipt of scholarships.
    - **Why Save It:** For records, future reference, and as proof of the scholarship if there are any discrepancies or requirements for maintaining the scholarship.
15. **Financial Aid Documentation**:
    - **Purpose**: Documentation related to your financial aid applications, including tax documents and bank statements, is crucial for verifying the information on your applications.
    - **Why Save It**: To facilitate any future verifications or corrections and for personal financial record-keeping.
16. **Visitation and Campus Tour Notes**:
    - **Purpose**: Notes from campus visits or tours help you remember specific details about each school.
    - **Why Save It**: Useful for comparing schools when deciding and preparing for campus life.

17. **College Essays and Personal Statements:**
    - **Purpose:** Essays and personal statements are integral to college applications, reflecting your personality and intellect.
    - **Why Save It:** They can be used as a starting point for future applications, including jobs, internships, and scholarships.
18. **College Acceptance Letters:**
    - **Purpose:** These are official notifications of your acceptance into a college or university.
    - **Why Save It:** For record-keeping, verification purposes, and as a personal milestone.
19. **Waitlist Notifications:**
    - **Purpose:** Notifications of waitlist status keep you informed about your chances of admission.
    - **Why Save It:** For reference, in case you need to respond or take further action regarding your waitlist status.
20. **Housing and Enrollment Information:**
    - **Purpose:** Documents related to housing and enrollment are necessary for finalizing your admission and securing your place at the college.
    - **Why Save It:** To ensure you meet all enrollment and housing requirements and deadlines.
21. **Transfer Credit Information:**
    - **Purpose:** For transfer students, information about transfer credits and course equivalencies is essential for understanding how previous work will be credited.
    - **Why Save It:** To plan your course schedule and ensure you meet graduation requirements.
22. **Correspondence with Admissions Offices:**
    - **Purpose:** This includes direct communication with admissions offices, such as application queries or additional information requests.

Why Save It: For records of what information has been requested and provided and to follow up on any outstanding questions or issues.

Keeping these documents organized and accessible ensures that you have all the necessary information at your fingertips throughout the college application and enrollment process. Having these readily available can significantly reduce the stress associated with the college application process and increase a student's chances of success.

Sample Thank You Letter For College Acceptance

Subject: Expressing Gratitude for the Acceptance to (College Name)

Dear (College Name) Admissions Committee,
I am very thankful to you for extending the opportunity for me to attend (college name). I am truly honored to have received an acceptance letter from your prestigious institution.

As I enter the final stretch of my senior year in high school, I am excited about the prospect of joining the (college name) community. Given the significance of this decision, it is essential for me to have a comprehensive view of my options before making my final commitment. Therefore, I plan to decide in late spring once I have almost completed my senior year and finalized my financial aid arrangements.

My acceptance to (college name) is a blessing, and I deeply appreciate your faith in me. I am enthusiastic about possibly being part of (college name)'s vibrant academic and social community.

Thank you once again for this incredible opportunity. I look forward to further exploring the possibilities that lie ahead and making my decision in the coming months.

Warm regards,

Your Name

Sample Letter To Include With Scholarship Application

Good afternoon. My name is (Your Name). I am a dedicated and current senior at (Your School) who is passionate about pursuing computer science. I am writing to submit my essay for the Peter Pan Scholarship and to express my gratitude for your generous support of young scholars like myself.

I have attached my scholarship essay, my transcript, and resume. I am incredibly thankful for the opportunity to be considered for this scholarship. My essay reflects my genuine passion and dedication to my chosen field. Once again, thank you for your unwavering support and commitment to empowering young scholars like myself.

Please don't hesitate to contact me if you need more information or have additional questions. Thank you for your time and consideration.

Warm regards,

Your Name

Final Thoughts:

As you reach the final pages of this journey, I want to express my heartfelt gratitude. Thank you for embarking on this adventure with me. Your support in purchasing this book means the world, and I sincerely hope you've found immense value within its pages.

This book was crafted with the intention of being your companion on the road to college acceptance. I trust that the insights, tips, and guidance provided have illuminated your path and equipped you with the tools needed for a successful journey.

Remember, this is not just a book; it's a shared experience. Your aspirations, dreams, and challenges are woven into the fabric of these words. As you navigate the intricate landscape of college applications, my wish for you is that this book has been a source of inspiration and practical guidance.

As you stand at the threshold of the college acceptance journey, I wish you every success. May your unique narrative shine brightly, captivating the hearts of admissions officers. May your ambitions take flight, and may you find the college that not only accepts you but embraces the exceptional individual that you are.

Thank you once again for being part of this journey. Here's to your success, dreams, and the exciting adventure ahead. Wishing you all the best in your pursuit of higher education and the fulfillment of your academic aspirations. Cheers to your future!

Katina Foster

Your Notes

Your Notes

Your Notes

Your Notes

Your Notes

Your Notes